Tim Lincecum

By Jeff Savage

AMAZING ATHLETES

Lerner Publications Company • Minneapolis

Lerner Publications Company
A division of Lerner Publishing Group, Inc.
241 First Avenue North
Minneapolis, MN 55401 U.S.A.

Website address: www.lernerbooks.com

Library of Congress Cataloging-in-Publication Data

Savage, Jeff, 1961–
    Tim Lincecum / by Jeff Savage.
        p.   cm. — (Amazing athletes)
    Includes index.
    ISBN 978-0-7613-8636-0 (lib. bdg. : alk. paper)
    1. Lincecum, Tim, 1874-—Juvenile literature. 2. Baseball players—United States—Biography—Juvenile literature. 3. Pitchers (Baseball)—United States—Biography—Juvenile literature. I. Title.
GV865.L535S38 2012
796.357092—dc23 [B]   2011035279

Manufactured in the United States of America
1 – BP – 12/31/11

TABLE OF CONTENTS

Tim Lincecum gets ready to throw a pitch against the Philadelphia Phillies.

BIG VICTORY

Tim Lincecum stood on the **pitcher's mound**. Tim is the **ace** pitcher for the San Francisco Giants. He is wire-thin with shaggy black hair. He looks more like a **bat boy** than a **major-league** pitcher.

The Giants needed a victory in this important 2011 game. They had lost three straight games to the Philadelphia Phillies. The Giants had to start winning if they wanted to make the **playoffs**. But the Phillies were hot. They had won nine games in a row. They owned the best record in baseball.

Tim had to pitch well to keep the Giants in the playoff race.

Tim threw a pitch. Phillies second baseman Chase Utley smacked the ball into center field. Roy Oswalt raced around third base and scored. The Phillies led, 1–0. Tim stayed calm. He knew how to pitch in big games. He was the starting pitcher in the 2009 **All-Star Game**. He pitched in two **World Series** games in 2010 and won them both.

The Giants scored a run in the fourth inning to tie the game. They scored again in the fifth inning and once more in the sixth to take a 3–1 lead. The Phillies could not come back.

In the eighth inning, Tim got the first two batters out. He needed just four more outs to win the game. Utley swung at a pitch and missed. He lost the grip on his bat. The bat

Tim throws right-handed but bats left-handed.

Tim *(center)* hands Chase Utley's bat back to him after the bat hit Tim in the knee.

skidded out to the mound and smacked Tim on the knee. Tim fell to the ground. He was hurt. Utley went out to the mound. Tim handed the bat back to him. Tim stayed in the game, but Utley hit his next pitch for a single. Tim was replaced by Brian Wilson. Wilson got the final outs to save the win for the Giants.

"This was a big victory for us," Tim said afterward. "I'm just glad I could help out."

Tim was born in Bellevue, Washington. Bellevue is near Seattle, Washington.

PUSHING HARD

Timothy Leroy Lincecum was born June 15, 1984, in Bellevue, Washington. He grew up in nearby Renton. His father, Chris, and his mother, Rebecca, raised Tim and his brother, Sean, together. Sean is four years older than Tim.

Tim learned to pitch in his backyard. His father first taught Sean how to pitch. Tim watched closely. By the age of five, Tim was practicing too. He learned the pitching motion that he still uses today. Tim kept his body from twisting for as long as possible. He took an extra long step toward home plate. All at once, he snapped his body around and threw the pitch. This motion gave him more power.

Tim was small for his age. As a freshman at Liberty High School in Renton, he was 4 feet 11 and weighed 85 pounds. He played sports anyway. He was the **quarterback** in football. He played **point guard** in basketball. But his favorite sport was baseball.

Tim has always been careful and neat. In high school, he lined his sports trophies on his shelf in perfect order. He kept his baseball jersey sleeves just above his elbows.

Tim practiced harder than his teammates. His brother later said, "There were always doubts, people saying, 'You're smaller than everyone else, so you have to do something extra.' Timmy pushed harder than anyone I know." As a sophomore, Tim reached 100 pounds. His junior year, he shot up to 5 feet 8. But he weighed just 125 pounds.

Tim's teammate Sean Webster said, "Timmy looked like he was swimming in his jersey, it was so big on him." Tim lifted heavy weights to make himself bigger and stronger. "I'm trying to get as much out of my body as I can," Tim said. "But I want to do it the right way." University of Washington baseball coach Ken Knutson heard about Tim. Coach Knutson was told that Tim could pitch for his team, the Huskies. The coach thought it was a joke. "He

Coach Knutson came to watch Tim play in high school.

looked like he was nine years old," said the coach. There was nothing funny about how Tim pitched. As a senior, he could throw a baseball 94 miles per hour. He led Liberty High to the state title. He was named state baseball player of the year.

The University of Washington Huskies play at Chaffey Field in Seattle.

Professional baseball **scouts** thought Tim was too small. He was finally picked in the 48th round of the 2003 Major League Baseball (MLB) **draft** by the Chicago Cubs. He was the 1,408th player picked.

Tim chose to go to college instead of joining the Cubs. He was offered a **scholarship** by Coach Knutson and the University of Washington. Tim agreed on one condition. The Huskies promised not to change Tim's unusual pitching motion.

Tim pitches for the Huskies during his freshman year of college.

THE FREAK

When Tim met his Huskies teammates, he thought, "Man, these guys are big." Tim weighed just 130 pounds as a college freshman, but he came up big in other ways. He threw the ball harder than anyone else on the team.

13

As a sophomore, Tim was named **Pac 10 Conference** Pitcher of the Year. But MLB scouts still didn't think he was good enough. He was not drafted until the 42nd round of the 2005 draft—this time by the Cleveland Indians. Once again, Tim chose college over joining MLB.

As a junior at the University of Washington,  he won the Golden Spikes Award as **amateur** baseball's best player. In three years, he had more strikeouts than any other pitcher in Pac 10 Conference history.

Tim had a great year pitching for the Huskies in 2006.

At the 2006 draft, six of the first seven teams chose pitchers. All of them passed on Tim. With the 10th overall pick, the Giants chose him. They paid him a $2 million **signing bonus**.

Tim was thrilled. He started pitching in the **minor leagues**. He faced three batters in his first game. He struck out all three. In 13 minor-league starts, he never lost a game. He allowed just seven runs. He struck out 104 batters.

Tim pitches for the Fresno (CA) Grizzlies in 2007.

In May 2007, the Giants called up Tim to the major leagues. His new teammates knew right away that Tim was going to be a special pitcher. The first thing they liked about him was his attitude. "He's a great kid who is smart, who is willing to learn, and who respects the game," said teammate Rich Aurilia.

When Tim joined the Giants, he had such a boyish face that sometimes he had to convince people that he was a player. Security guards at stadiums thought he was a kid trying to sneak into the locker room.

Giants teammate Rich Aurilia *(below)* saw how good Tim could be.

Tim jokes with teammates during a game in 2007.

Tim was different in many ways. He sang songs as he walked around the locker room. His teammates called him the human juke box. He waved a towel in the **dugout** and cheered for his teammates. Many starting pitchers wrap a bag of ice on their throwing shoulder or elbow after they pitch. Tim did not do this. His father taught him not to use ice. Players wondered how a player Tim's size could be so powerful. Soon he had a new nickname—the Freak.

Tim started strong in 2008.

CY YOUNG WINNER

Tim's first full season with the Giants was 2008. He was already the team's ace. He threw several types of pitches. He threw his **fastball** exactly where he aimed. He had a big **curveball** and a tricky **changeup**. With the Giants, he learned to throw a **slider**. Opponents said that batting against Tim seemed unfair. "He has three almost unhittable pitches," St. Louis Cardinals slugger Lance Berkman said. "When he throws those off-speed pitches where he wants, you've got no chance."

Midway through the season, Tim was chosen to pitch in his first All-Star Game. The day of the game, he was sent to the hospital with the flu. He missed the game. Tim had never played a full major-league season. He was smaller than most MLB players. Some wondered if he would wear down.

Tim is small for a major-league pitcher. But his size has never stopped him from striking out hitters.

Tim stayed strong. In the last month of the season, he pitched all nine innings of a major-league game for the first time. He struck out 12 batters and allowed just four singles in a 7–0 win over the San Diego Padres. In the ninth inning, his fastball was still averaging 95 miles per hour. Usually, a pitcher's speed goes down in the last innings. He threw 138 pitches in the game, the most by any pitcher in a game that year.

Ten days later against the Colorado Rockies, Tim broke San Francisco's single-season strikeout record. He finished with 265 strikeouts, tops in the **National League (NL)**. Tim's final record was 18–5. He won the NL Cy Young Award as the best pitcher.

Tim's father, Chris, has a show on the radio in San Francisco called *Father Knows Best*. Chris talks about his son Tim and Giants baseball.

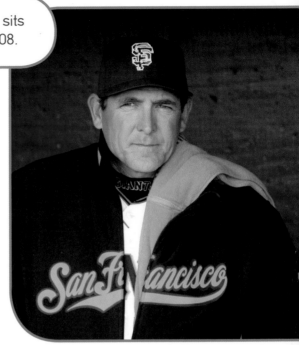

Giants pitching coach Dave Righetti works closely with his pitchers. But the coach knew Tim was special. "I treat Timmy differently," Righetti admitted. "I leave him alone." The Giants knew that Tim's unusual pitching motion was a big part of his success.

Tim was brilliant again in 2009. In a game against the Cardinals, he threw a two-hit shutout. That game was part of a scoreless streak of 29 innings for Tim. He was named the starting pitcher for the All-Star Game. In two innings, he allowed one earned run.

Later that season against the Pittsburgh Pirates, Tim struck out 15 batters, a career high. He finished the year with a 15–7 record and led the league in strikeouts again. He won his second straight Cy Young Award. Tim was the first player in major-league history to receive the award after his first two full seasons. He was proud to win this trophy again. But Tim cared more for his team. His goal was to win the biggest team prize in baseball—the World Series trophy.

Tim and his dad hold Tim's two Cy Young Awards during the presentation for the 2009 award.

Tim talks to catcher Buster Posey during a game in 2010.

WORLD SERIES CHAMPS

Tim blazed to a 5–0 start in 2010. The team's other pitchers also played well and helped give the Giants a chance to get into the playoffs. But the team struggled to score runs. They made the playoffs on the final day of the regular season, beating the Padres by just two games.

Tim and the Giants faced the Atlanta Braves in Game 1 of the NL Division Series. It was all they needed. Tim allowed just two hits and one walk in nine innings. San Francisco went on to win the series in four games.

The Giants met the Philadelphia Phillies in the NL Championship Series. The winning team would move on to the World Series. Tim faced superstar Roy Halladay in Game 1 in Philadelphia. Cody Ross hit two home runs for the Giants. Tim kept his

Tim focuses on his next pitch after giving up a home run to the Phillies in Game 1.

team in front by striking out eight batters. The Giants won the game, 4–3, and took the series in six games.

The Giants played the Texas Rangers in the 2010 World Series. In Game 1, Tim pitched the Giants to victory with more than five strong innings. In Game 5, San Francisco needed just one more win to capture its first world title. It was Tim's turn to pitch again.

Tim warms up for Game 5 of the 2010 World Series.

With millions of people watching, Tim tried to stay calm. "I just took more deep breaths," he said. Neither team scored through seven innings. In the top of the eighth inning, Edgar Renteria blasted a three-run home run for the Giants. Tim gave up a solo homer in the bottom of the inning. It was just the third hit he allowed all night.

Wilson saved the game in the ninth inning for a 3–1 win. The Giants celebrated on the field and in the locker room.

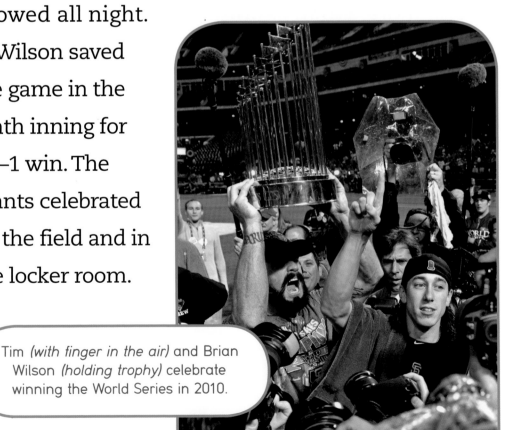

Tim *(with finger in the air)* and Brian Wilson *(holding trophy)* celebrate winning the World Series in 2010.

Asked how he felt, Tim said, "Excited! Exhausted!"

In 2011 the Giants were in the playoff hunt again. Tim showed that he was ready for another great season when he carried a no-hitter into the seventh inning at Colorado. The Giants beat the Rockies, 8–1.

"He's a big pressure pitcher," said Giants manager Bruce Bochy. "When our team needs a lift, Timmy carries us." But Tim couldn't carry his team all the way in 2011. San Francisco finished the season in second place behind the Arizona Diamondbacks and missed the playoffs.

After a game in 2011, Giants fan Bryan Stow was seriously injured outside Dodger Stadium in Los Angeles, California. Tim gave $25,000 to the Bryan Stow Fund to help pay medical bills.

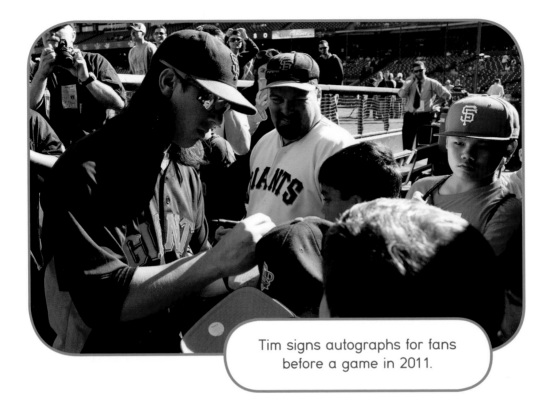

Tim signs autographs for fans before a game in 2011.

Tim is so strong he can walk across a baseball field on his hands. While standing still, he can spring into a backflip. He has the body of a gymnast. But Tim's real secret is his willpower. "My dad pushed me," he said. "And then I pushed myself. If I would have listened to all those people who said I was too small, I probably wouldn't be here."

Selected Career Highlights

2011 Named to the NL All-Star team

2010 Led the Giants to the World Series title
Led NL in strikeouts with 231
Set a major-league record for most
   strikeouts in the first four seasons
Set a Giants record for victories (4) in a
   single postseason
Named to the NL All-Star team

2009 Won the Cy Young Award as the NL's top
   pitcher
Led the NL in strikeouts with 261
Named the starting pitcher for the NL at
   the All-Star Game

2008 Won the Cy Young Award as the NL's top
   pitcher
Led Major League Baseball in strikeouts
   with 265
Allowed the fewest hits per nine innings
   among NL pitchers
Ranked second in the NL in earned run
   average (2.62)
Named to the NL All-Star team

2007 Ranked second in the NL in strikeouts per nine innings (9.23)

2006 Drafted in the 1st round by the San Francisco Giants
Named Pac 10 Conference Pitcher of the Year
Set Pac 10 Conference record for career strikeouts

2005 Named Pac 10 Conference Pitcher of the Year
Drafted in the 42nd round by the Cleveland Indians (but did not sign)

2004 Joined the University of Washington baseball team

2003 Named Washington's Gatorade High School Player of the Year
Led Liberty High to a state championship
Drafted in the 48th round by the Chicago Cubs (but did not sign)

Glossary

ace: in baseball, the pitcher who is the top starter on a team

All-Star Game: a game held midway through the Major League Baseball season featuring the best players in each league

amateur: players who do not play professionally for money, such as high school or college players

bat boy: usually a younger person whose main job is to pick up the player's bat near home plate and return it to the dugout after the player has batted

changeup: a pitch thrown in a similar motion as a fastball but at a slower speed

curveball: a slower pitch that dives downward as it approaches home plate

draft: a yearly event in which players from a group are chosen by teams

dugout: a covered area with a long bench along either side of a baseball field where players sit during a game

fastball: a fast pitch that usually travels straight

major league: the top level of professional baseball

minor leagues: a series of teams below the top major-league team in which players gain experience and improve their skills

National League (NL): one of baseball's two major leagues. The National League includes the San Francisco Giants, the San Diego Padres, the St. Louis Cardinals, and others.

Pac 10 Conference: a group of 10 college teams from the western United States. (The conference was expanded to 12 teams in 2011.)

pitcher's mound: a dirt hill in the shape of a circle about 60 feet from home plate on which the pitcher stands

playoffs: a series of games held every year to decide a champion

point guard: a player on a basketball team who directs the other players and who handles the ball most of the time

quarterback: a player on a football team whose main job is to call the plays and throw passes

scholarship: in athletics, money or other aid given to a student in exchange for playing a sport

scouts: experts who watch players in high school and college to determine if they should choose them in baseball's draft

signing bonus: a sum of money given to a player as a reward for signing a contract

slider: a pitch that drops downward and sideways as it approaches home plate

World Series: the final round of the playoffs in which the winners of the American League and the National League compete until one team wins four games

Further Reading & Websites

Boone, Mary. *Tim Lincecum*. Hockessin, DE: Mitchell Lane Publishers, 2012.

Glaser, Jason. *Tim Lincecum*. New York: Gareth Stevens Publishing, 2012.

Kennedy, Mike, and Mark Stewart. *Long Ball: The Legend and Lore of the Home Run*. Minneapolis: Millbrook Press, 2006.

Savage, Jeff. *Roy Halladay*. Minneapolis: Lerner Publications Company, 2011.

The Official Site of Major League Baseball
http://www.mlb.com
Major League Baseball's official website provides fans with the latest scores and game schedules, as well as information on players, teams, and baseball history.

The Official Site of the San Francisco Giants
http://sanfrancisco.giants.mlb.com/index.jsp?c_id=sf
The San Francisco Giants official site includes team schedules and game results, late-breaking news, biographies of Tim Lincecum and other players and coaches, and much more.

Sports Illustrated Kids
http://www.sikids.com
The *Sports Illustrated Kids* website covers all sports, including baseball.

Index

Photo Acknowledgments

The images in this book are used with the permission of: © Michael
Zagaris/Getty Images, p. 4; © Jason O. Watson/US Presswire, p. 5; © Thearon
W. Henderson/Getty Images, p. 7; © David Barnes/Photodisc/Getty Images,
p. 8; AP Photo/Ralph Radford, p. 11, 13; © Eric and Wendy Pastore, www.
digitalballparks.com, p. 12; AP Photo/Kevin P. Casey, p. 14; © Don Davis
Photography, p. 15; © Chris Talley/Cal Sport Media/ZUMA Press, p. 16; © Brad
Mangin/MLB Photos via Getty Images, p. 17; © Paul Jasienski/Getty Images,
p. 18; © Matthew O'Haren/CORBIS, p. 19; AP Photo/Jeff Chiu, p. 21; AP Photo/
Ben Margot, p. 22; © Ezra Shaw/Getty Images, p. 23; © Chris McGrath/Getty
Images, p. 24; © Lance Iversen/CORBIS, p. 25; © Scott Rovak/US Presswire,
p. 26; © Tony Medina/Getty Images, p. 28; © Brad Mangin/Getty Images, p. 29.

Front cover: © Rob Carr/Getty Images Sport.

Main body text set in Caecilia LT Std 55 Roman 16/28. Typeface provided by
Linotype AG.